Foreword

By Andrew Kent, Port Manager

The Port of Southampton has a rich history stretching back many centuries, although, it has been over the last 160 years that the real development of commercial shipping and cargo handling facilities in Southampton has taken place. In that time, the Port has played an important role in the economic fortunes of the Region, generating considerable prosperity and employment.

The Port today is a particular success story, handling around 7% of all UK International trade, and growing steadily year after year. This growth and prosperity has been the result of major port developments undertaken over the years, all requiring a great deal of foresight, a degree of risk and, of course, hard work. As a result, many thousands of people who live and work in and around the Port, and their families, now depend on its activities for their livelihoods.

Progress such as this does not come by accident. It depends in part on Southampton's strategic location and deep water, but even these natural advantages are now not enough, in this era of huge ships trading on global routes, if Southampton is to continue to prosper.

Major investment is needed to keep pace with the changing requirements of world trade, and if the Port of Southampton is to continue as one of Europe's international trading centres, it is vital to carry forward, as we are doing today, the development process started by our predecessors nearly 160 years ago. This will ensure that the Port continues to bring prosperity not only to the Region, but to the UK as a whole.

Pictori
or
Southampton
Docks

Revised Edition

By Bert Moody

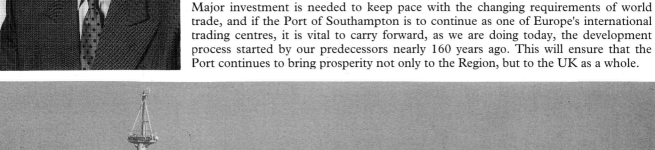

Above: Southampton is one of the UK's busiest and most diverse Ports.
Trevor Coppack
Front cover: P&O's new *Oriana* passes Cunard's *QE2* at Dock Head.
Back cover: A window on the past; *Queen Elizabeth* in the Port following a trans-Atlantic run. *ABP*

Published by

Waterfront Publications

A division of Kingfisher Productions
The Dalesmade Centre, Watershed Mill, Settle, North Yorkshire BD24 9LR
Copyright 1998 ISBN 0 946184 82 8 Third Edition

This book is a revised edition of the very successful publication produced in 1988 to mark the 150th anniversary of Southampton Docks. It was also revised in 1994 as 'A Pictorial History of Southampton Docks'.

It was on the 12th October 1838 that the foundation stone was laid for the construction of a dock in Southampton - the beginnings of one of the most important ports in the United Kingdom. Its natural attributes, including a small tidal range, prolonged periods of high waters, the unusual 'double' tides and its close connections with the continent, have all helped to create the title eventually given to the Port - THE GATEWAY TO THE WORLD.

For many years the massive movement of passengers through the Port to or from all parts of the world fully justified that title. This cannot be said of today, although the present-day cruise liners passing through Southampton still serve many parts of the world and are a very important part of the Port scene.

Thanks are due to many people who have assisted in various ways with information and photographs, particularly Associated British Ports, the staff at Southampton Civic Centre Reference Library, Southampton Museums and Roger Hardingham of Waterfront Publications.

Southampton Docks – 25th July 1956 a year in which 626, 856 passengers passed through the port. On the Itchen Quays are the troopship *Nevasa*, the *San Miguel*, Home Lines' *Homeric* and another troopship – *Dunera*. In the Empress Dock are Fyffes *Corrales* at 24/5 berths and a naval tanker *Wave Conqueror* at 26/7 berths under repair, while in No. 5 drydock is Brocklebank's *Mahronda*. P&O's *Stratheden* is at 40 berth on the River Test and in the Ocean Dock are the *Queen Elizabeth*, the *Karadeniz* at 45 berth, P&O's *Iberia* at 46 and Greek Line's *Neptunia* at 47 berth with the troopship *Dilwara* in No. 6 drydock. In the Western Docks is Union Castle's *Carnarvon Castle*, followed by the *Queen Mary*, *Athlone Castle* and the *United States*.   *Author's Collection*

The Early Years

The first real attempt to provide a railway between London and Southampton was made at a meeting held in Southampton in October 1830, and as a result a prospectus was issued in respect of the Southampton, London & Branch Railway Company. It was, however, felt that linked with the provision of the railway there should be the construction of a dock, and at a meeting held on 26th February 1831 it was agreed to form the Southampton, London & Branch Railway and Dock Company. Initially very little interest was created locally and about a year later, in January 1832, the proposal was revised and the projected dock scheme was omitted, being left for that part of the scheme to be developed as a separate company.

At the time Southampton's trade was mostly coastwise or continental, and what quays were available were dry at low water, with the exception of the Royal Victoria Pier, which was constructed in 1833. But this was inadequate for the larger ships that were then being built there was no accommodation for the repair of such vessels.

In May 1836 an Act authorising the newly formed Southampton Dock Company to construct a dock at Southampton was passed by Parliament, the authorised capital being £350,000. At a meeting of some fifty businessmen from London, Liverpool, Manchester and Southampton, held on 16th August 1836 at the George & Vulture Tavern, a well known hostelry in Lombard Street, London, the chairman of the company announced that the directors had acquired 216 acres of mudlands adjoining the Town Quay at Southampton at a cost of £5,000. The original plans provided for four docks giving access to the deeper water of the main tidal channel, but initially it was the intention to construct just one closed (non-tidal) dock. Locally the proposals brought forth a spate of complaints - dramatic debates took place in the Town Council and grave doubts were expressed as to whether: 'A set of unknown and irresponsible individuals could turn so great an extent of land to beneficial purposes'.

The Engineer engaged by the Dock Company was Francis Giles, who had carried out the initial surveys for the construction of the London and Southampton Railway, but owing to various difficulties he was replaced by the railway company with Joseph Locke. Giles remained engineer for the Dock Company until just before his death in 1846, when his son, Alfred, became Docks Engineer, serving the Dock Company for many years.

Preparation for the dock went ahead and two years after the passing of the Act a great day for Southampton arrived with the laying of the foundation stone. This event took place on 12th October 1838 – the year of Queen Victoria's Coronation – and no doubt many of those who had been loudest in voicing their opposition before, now joined wholeheartedly in celebrating the occasion. According to a newspaper report of that day there was

Laying of the foundation stone – 12th October 1838. An engraving of that momentous occasion. The stone was laid where the north and west boundaries of the area met, close by what eventually became No. 1 Gate, and about eighty yards west of the site on which the docks Post Office was subsequently built. In the engraving Gods House can be seen in the background. Even in those days the authorities showed considerable foresight for the first dock, the Outer Dock, was constructed some distance away on the River Itchen. *Associated British Ports*

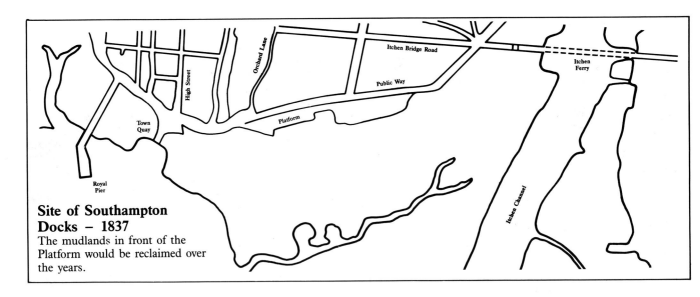

Site of Southampton Docks – 1837
The mudlands in front of the Platform would be reclaimed over the years.

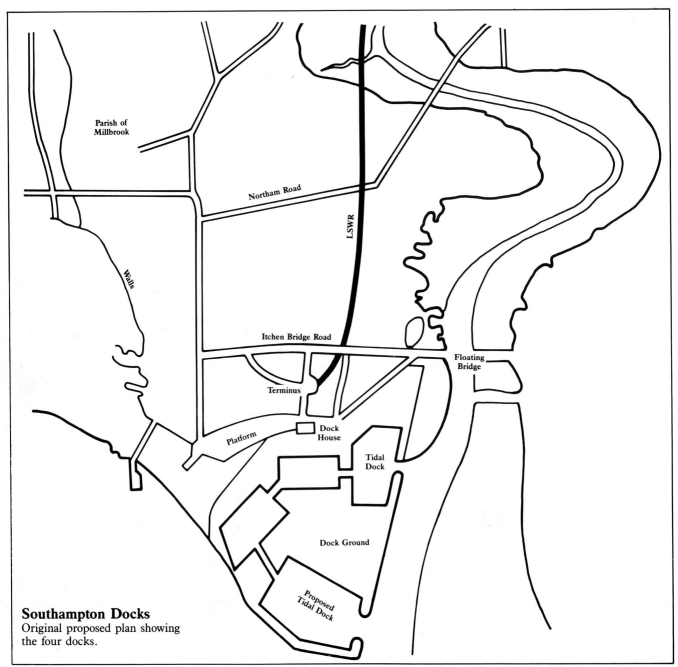

Southampton Docks
Original proposed plan showing the four docks.

The foundation stone which actually consists of two stones, now stands on a temporary site not very far from Dock House. It has, however, had a somewhat mysterious life for it would seem that during the 19th century the stone was forgotten and it was eventually discovered in June 1900 by a party of workmen in its original position embedded in a concrete wall. A newspaper report of 1900 stated that it had been decided to raise and inscribe the stone, but although it was raised it was never inscribed and its whereabouts were soon forgotten again. It was not until 1948 when it was re-discovered and was eventually erected on a plinth near the north end of the Ocean Terminal, as shown in the above picture. It remained here until the demolition of the Ocean Terminal in 1983. *Author*

much ceremony and the greatest assembly of gratified spectators that had, till then, gathered in the Town:

> 'The interest was immense. At an early hour of the morning, the bells of the parish churches rang their merry peals, and announced to the town that the preparation had commenced, vessels in the harbour were dressed in colours, steamers manned their yards, and all the town and neighbourhood put on that appearance of gaiety which the occasion deserved. The number of strangers that flocked into the town from all quarters was immense, and as the hour for the appearance of the procession approached all the shops closed.'

Headed by the Mayor and Corporation and including many Masonic Brethren in regalia, the imposing cavalcade wound its way through the town to the appointed place near the harbour where about 20,000 people (the population of the town was then near that figure) had taken up positions to witness the ceremony about to be performed with Masonic honours, by the Deputy Provincial Grand Master of Hampshire, Sir Lucius Curtis. Upon the request of Joseph Liggins, the chairman of the Dock Company, and after the blessing bestowed by the Masonic Chaplain, the Deputy Provincial Grand Master laid down the stone saying – 'May the Great Architect of the Universe enable us successfully to carry on and finish the work of which we have now laid the foundation stone and every other undertaking that may tend to the advantage of the Town County of Southampton and its harbour. May he be a guard and protection to them and may they long be preserved from peril and decay'. A royal salute was fired, after which the procession reformed and proceeded back to the town.

An artist's impression of Southampton Docks in the 1850s showing the Outer and Inner Docks and typical ships of the period. In the background are the spires of St. Michael's and Holy Rood churches, whilst on the left of the Outer Dock can be seen the entrances to three of Southampton's drydocks, opened in 1846, 1847 and 1854 respectively. These drydocks were capable of accommodating the largest ships of their day.

An early photograph of the docks taken about 1872/3 from the top of the South Western Hotel. Dock House, minus its Canute Road entrance, can be clearly seen and the small house in front is believed to have been occupied by the Docks Engineer of those days. Maritime Chambers was built on that site in 1899. Both the Inner and Outer Docks are well occupied with shipping.

Associated British Ports

It was under the most auspicious influence that the great venture of Southampton Docks was inaugurated. Changing circumstances were affecting the maritime affairs of England. For one thing the great trade routes from the Far East were gaining a new importance, and it was seen that whereas these tended to operate from the Port of London, the shorter route to Southampton would not only be beneficial to the Hampshire port, but eliminate the risks entailed by the passage through the then perilous Straits of Dover. The new and general adoption of the growing railway transport would at the same time expedite the forwarding of merchandise to various parts of the Kingdom with a facility hitherto unknown.

In 1839 the name of the railway company was changed from the London and Southampton Railway to the London & South Western Railway, and the line to Southampton from London Nine Elms (Waterloo station was not opened until 1848) was opened throughout on the 11th May 1840.

Another factor, namely the revolution which was already evident in shipping commerce as a result of the advent of the steamship, was causing the directors of the Dock Company to modify their original plans. Instead of continuing with the building of a closed dock, they proceeded with the construction of a tidal or open dock, which offered greater advantages in the matter of accommodating steamships. This Tidal Dock, which later became known as the Outer Dock, covered 16 acres in extent, and was so far towards completion by August 1842 that on the 29th of that month it was opened to accommodate two vessels of the Peninsular & Oriental Steam Navigation Company, the *Tagus* of 780 tons and the *Liverpool* of 450 tons. This company had used the harbour at Southampton since 1840, and these two steamers were thus the first to be berthed in the docks. In conjunction with the construction of this dock the railway line was extended across Canute Road, and so it was possible, on this inaugural occasion, to discharge cargo from the two ships into railway wagons for conveyance direct to London. On the 1st July of the following year the dock was opened to general trade.

In 1839 the Royal Mail Steam Packet Company was formed and in the following year a contract was signed with the government for the conveyance of mails to and from Great Britain and the West Indies, and North and South America, requiring the provision of fourteen steamships. The company examined the merits of various south coast ports and commissioned the engineer, John Smeaton, to examine and report upon the suitability of Southampton as a terminal port for their steamers. His report was favourable and ended with the words: 'Southampton as a Steam Boat station is unrivalled in England', and so it came about that the Royal Mail Steam Packet Company commenced to use Southampton and continued to do so for the next 150 years.

With the opening of the Outer Dock, Southampton was being used by many important steamers, and so the need for providing dry dock accommodation soon became a pressing one. To meet these needs the Southampton Dock Company had constructed between 1846 and 1854 three graving or dry docks, the first of these being completed in 1846. It was 400 feet in length and 21 feet deep, and could receive the largest ships of the day. The first vessel to enter the drydock was the Royal Mail Steam Packet's *Forth* 1939 tons on 27th July 1846 for the purpose of being coppered.

Prior to the arrival of the railway in Southampton, paddle steamers operated from the Royal Pier to the Channel Islands and Le Havre, but the directors of the London & South Western Railway soon appreciated that the steamers could provide additional traffic for their trains. However, at the time the railway companies in Britain were not permitted by law to own steamers, so in 1842 some of the directors promoted a new shipping company – the South Western S.N. Company and their first steamer, built in 1843, was appropriately named *South Western*. In 1846 that company was reformed and became the New South Western Steam Packet Company. It was not until August 1860 that Parliament gave authority for the L&SWR to operate steamships and the New South Western SP Company was taken over in July 1862. Thus developed the railway-owned cross channel steamer services, which continued from Southampton until the early 1960s.

The increasing substitution of the steamship for the sailing vessel and the connection of Southampton to all parts of the country by means of the railway, rapidly advanced the shipping trade of the port to such an extent that the necessity for additional docks soon became apparent. This led to the directors of the Dock Company deciding to proceed with the construction of a second dock. This became known as the Inner Dock and was the only closed or non-tidal dock on the whole estate. The Inner Dock covered a water area of 10 acres with an entrance originally 46 feet wide. The need for this new dock was such that it was opened to shipping, although incomplete, at the end of 1851. The size of the vessels, however, continued to increase so it was necessary to enlarge the width of the entrance to the dock and deepen it. The work was completed, and the dock was re-opened for trade on 25th May 1859, when the inhabitants of the town were admitted to witness the berthing of the P & O S N Company's *Pera*, 2,014 gross tons, the first vessel to use the dock after the reconstruction.

In the spring of 1854 the Crimea War broke out and this had an immediate effect on Southampton for a large number of steamers using the port were requisitioned to convey troops and horses, together with supplies, to the scene of activities. The P & O Company alone transported about 90,000 men and between 15,000 and 20,000 horses. Arising from the Crimean War there was a development which eventually resulted in one of the major shipping links with the port being established. In 1853 a new steamship company, the Union Steam Collier Company, had commenced a coal-carrying trade between Southampton and the Mediterranean, but upon the outbreak of hostilities its ships had been chartered for carrying stores etc. Soon after the end of the war the company changed its name to the Union Steam Ship Company and entered the South African trade. The Government contracted a monthly mail service to South African ports and on the 15th September 1857, there set out from the port the *Dane* of 530 tons, on the inaugural voyage of the new service. This vessel was the pioneer of many ships of the Union Line which amalgamated with the Castle Line in 1900 to form the Union Castle Mail Steamship Company whose weekly mail service from Southampton to South Africa was maintained until September 1977.

Various continental shipping companies started to use Southampton as an intermediary port of call en route from Germany to New York, these being the Hamburg America Line in 1857 and Norddeutscher Lloyd in 1858. Ships of the Nederland Steamship Company and the Java Steamship Company (later to become Rotterdam Lloyd) commenced to call on their way to and from the Dutch East Indies during the 1870s.

With the increased trade, the demand for more quays became acute, and so the construction along the River Itchen, extending to nearly 2,000 feet, was commenced in 1873 and completed in 1876. The P & O S N Company, which had regularly used the port since the opening of the first dock, decided in 1875, partly due to pressure from London merchants and also due to the limitations of the accommodation at Southampton, to transfer their operations to London, although some of their ships continued to call at Southampton for passengers and mails until 1881. Despite this serious loss the amount of shipping tonnage entering the Docks in 1876 actually exceeded that of 1874 which speaks much for the continued general progress of the port.

In 1879 a fourth drydock was completed, located alongside the River Itchen. Initially this dock was required mainly for the overhaul of Union Steamship Company's vessels. The size of ocean going steamers continued to increase and so the demand for more and larger docks continued, although another deep water dock was planned, the project could not be carried out for a number of years. The expansion which had taken place so far had placed a burden on the Dock Company's finances, with gradually mounting expenditure on account of repairs and improvements, necessitating frequent calls for increase in capital, and unfortunately such capital was becoming more and more difficult to obtain. For one thing trade depression throughout the country in the years following 1880 reduced traffic receipts considerably. A greatly increased assessment of the Docks Estate for local rating purposes also laid an additional heavy burden upon the revenue at that time. Eventually, the Dock Company, with sanction from Parliament, entered into an arrangement with the London & South Western Railway Company for a loan of £250,000 to enable the construction of the new deep water dock to go ahead. Work was immediately commenced and on the 26th July 1890 Her Majesty Queen Victoria opened the 'Empress Dock', providing an additional quay frontage of 3,800 feet. A forecast of the important position Southampton was to hold in the shipping world was possible even at that time, for with the opening of the Empress Dock Southampton became the only port in Great Britain at which vessels of the deepest draught could enter or leave at any state of the tide.

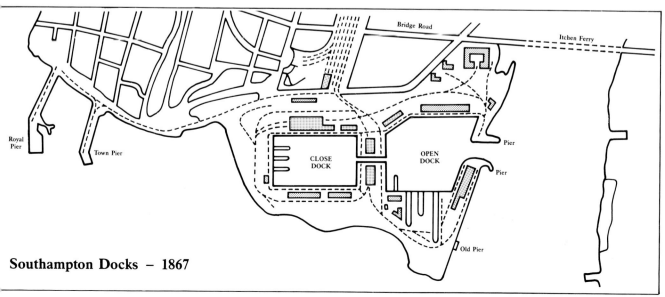

Southampton Docks – 1867

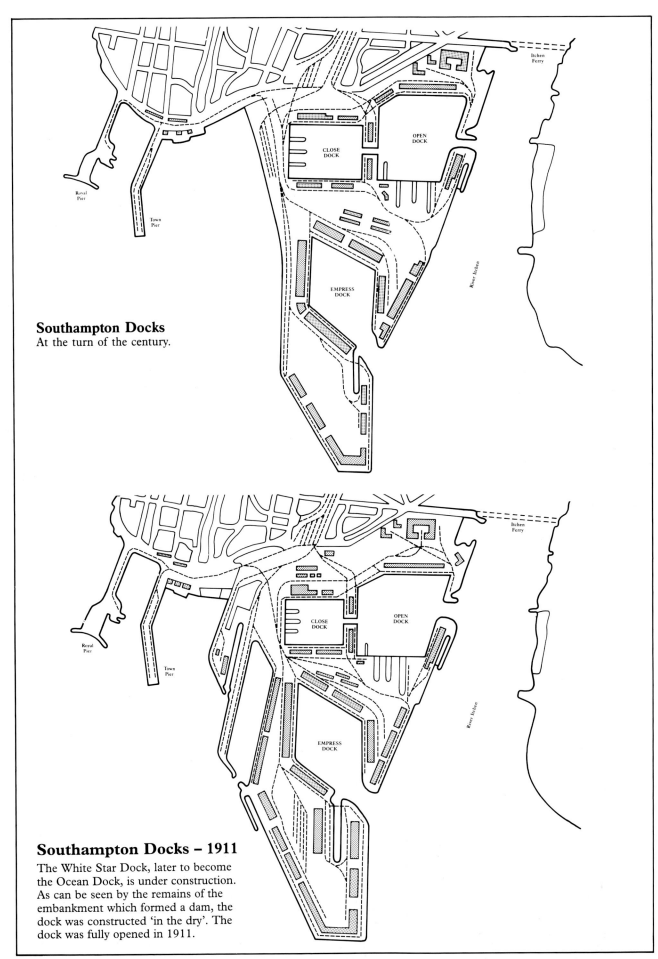

Southampton Docks
At the turn of the century.

Southampton Docks – 1911
The White Star Dock, later to become the Ocean Dock, is under construction. As can be seen by the remains of the embankment which formed a dam, the dock was constructed 'in the dry'. The dock was fully opened in 1911.

The Outer Dock. This well known photograph of the Outer Dock by F.G.O. Stuart, taken about 1888/9, has been included to emphasise how limited the accommodation in the docks was at that time – berthing space was obviously at a premium – the Empress Dock was still under construction. In the foreground can be seen the entrances to Nos. 1, 2 and 3 drydocks, and the large two funnelled vessel on the move is the P&OSN Company's *Arcadia*. In the background can be seen the chimney of the old sugar warehouse, and also the old Royal Mail Steam Packet Company's workshops (later to be taken over by Harland & Wolff). *Author's Collection*

Empress Dock in the early 1900s showing ships of three of the main shipping companies then operating from the port. On the left is the bow of a Royal Mail Steam Packet Company's ship, in the centre on the move is the *New York* or *Philadelphia* of the American Line and on the right one of the vessels owned by Union Castle Mail S.S. Company. *P. Gosling Collection*

Change of Ownership

The loan from the railway company did not considerably improve the financial position of the Dock Company, and eventually further discussions took place resulting in the whole dock undertaking passing into the hands of the London & South Western Railway Company on 1st November 1892, the agreed purchase price being £1,360,000. Thus what had been proposed in 1831 was finally accomplished sixty one years later.

Even before the completion of the Empress Dock, there were indications that the provision of more accommodation might influence other shipping interests to favour Southampton and this was soon confirmed. In 1893 an important shipping concern, the American Line, transferred their New York mail service from Liverpool to Southampton, and this commenced the big movement of North Atlantic express services from Merseyside to Southampton. The first steamer of the American Line to call was the three funnelled *New York* of 10,498 gross tons, on 4th March 1893, and at that time this vessel held the record for the fastest Atlantic crossing - eastbound Sandy Hook to Liverpool of 5 days 19 hours 57 minutes.

For many years the movement of troops from this country to overseas stations, particular to India, was under the control of the Admiralty, but in the early 1890s a new system was introduced whereby vessels were hired from various shipping companies; and with this change Southampton, in 1894, became the principal port for peacetime troopship movements, a state of affairs which prevailed up to the end of trooping by sea in December 1962. The importance of Southampton for troop movements was also fully demonstrated during the South African war of 1899 - 1902. The close connection by rail from Aldershot direct to the ship side was so advantageous that troops were

Early stages in the construction of No. 6 (Trafalgar) drydock – about 1901 – the work being carried out by John Aird & Company. Much of the earth removed was loaded into railway wagons and taken to the Western Esplanade, being used to reclaim land on which Pirelli General Cable Works was eventually built. In the background on the right can be seen the South Western Hotel and to the left Queens Terrace. The drydock was opened on 21st October 1905 by the Marquis of Winchester, Lord Lieutenant of the County, in the presence of a large gathering of dignitaries.

Author's Collection

UNION ⚑ LINE.

FOR THE

South African Gold and Diamond Fields, Mashonaland and Matabeleland.

WEEKLY DEPARTURES FROM SOUTHAMPTON.

Fleet:

	TONS.
NORMAN	7,537
SCOT .	6,850
GUELPH	4,916
GREEK .	4,747
GAUL .	4,744
GOTH .	4,738
MEXICAN .	4,661
MOOR . .	4,464
TARTAR .	4,425

(Twin Screw.)

R.M. Twin-Screw S.S. "Norman," 7,537 Tons.

Fleet:

	TONS.
ATHENIAN .	3,882
TROJAN .	3,652
SPARTAN .	3,403
PRETORIA .	3,303
ARAB . .	3,192
GERMAN .	3,007
SAXON . .	462
NATAL . .	158
CARNARVON	103

Union Line Express from Waterloo every Saturday.

The **Royal Mail** and **Intermediate** Steamers sail from **Southampton** on alternate **Saturdays,** making a **Weekly Service** to **South** and **East African** Ports.

The **Mail** Steamers call at **Madeira,** and the **Intermediate** Steamers at **Lisbon** and **Teneriffe,** unless Quarantine restrictions interfere.

Connection with Steamers of the **German East African Line** for **East African** Ports.

FARES FROM TEN GUINEAS.

Free Railway Tickets from London & Plymouth to Southampton.

Cheap Return Rail Tickets to Southampton for Passengers' Friends.

RETURN TICKETS ISSUED TO ALL PORTS.
SURGEON AND STEWARDESSES CARRIED.
SUPERIOR ACCOMMODATION AND CUISINE.

For Handbook and all Information apply to :—

THE UNION STEAM SHIP COMPANY, Ltd.,

CANUTE ROAD, SOUTHAMPTON ; 14, COCKSPUR STREET, LONDON, S.W. ;

AND

South African House, 94 to 96, Bishopsgate Street Within, London, E.C.

An 1895 advertisement for the Union Line's sailings from Southampton to South Africa. The Union Line amalgamated with the Castle Line in 1900 to form the Union Castle Mail S.S. Company.　　*Author's Collection*

A very early photograph of the completed Trafalgar Dock showing the three masted sailing vessel *Sylvia* in the dock. It will be noted that the Harland & Wolff Works had not yet been constructed.
Southampton City Museums

A later photograph of the drydock showing the White Star Line's *Teutonic* in the drydock.
Pamlin Prints

The Inner Dock about 1910 with the Royal Mail Steam Packet Company's *Nile* and *Danube* laid up. Also to be seen is a three masted schooner yacht, a large steam yacht and, partly hidden behind the steamers, a four masted barque. *Author's Collection*

The Inner Dock about 1920. Of the two vessels on the quayside, the one on the right is alongside the grain unloading equipment which then existed in that dock. The Inner Dock was the only non-tidal basin on the whole estate, the entrance lock can be clearly seen in the foreground. *Authors collection*

constantly embarked without a hitch. On 20th October 1899 five troopships were despatched between 2.30 pm and 4.30 pm and no fewer than nine vessels were berthed and dealt with simultaneously, in addition to the ordinary shipping of the port. During the South African War period, 419 transports left Southampton and 476 arrived with troops. The number of men passing through the port was 25,384 officers, 502,616 men and 27,922 horses, besides women and children, together with an enormous quantity of baggage and stores etc.

The year 1895 saw the opening of another drydock, at the time the largest in the world - it was opened on 3rd August 1895 by HRH The Prince of Wales (later to become King Edward VII) and named 'The Prince of Wales Dock (No. 5 drydock)'.

The London & South Western Railway Company continued with a vigorous policy of modernisation – electricity was substituted for gas, new warehouses were erected and a modern cranage system was installed. The approach channel to the docks was also dredged to a depth of 30 feet at low water (spring tides).

By the end of 1895 all the quays on the River Itchen were completed up to dockhead and work was then started on a portion facing the River Test. On this latter area in 1901, was opened the large cold store owned by the International Cold Store & Ice Company.

In 1898, to mark the progress made in the sixty years since the laying of the foundation stone, an appropriate ceremony was held when a coping stone, suitably inscribed, was laid at the west end of 37 berth at Dockhead.

On the centenary of the Battle of Trafalgar, on the 21st October 1905, the sixth drydock was opened and to mark the occasion it was named Trafalgar Dock. Within six years, however, alterations were to be made to enlarge this drydock.

Two years later, in 1907, the White Star Line transferred their North Atlantic express service from Liverpool to Southampton and on the 29th May their *Adriatic* arrived with 996 passengers. Her arrival clearly indicated how the size of the fast liners was increasing; the *New York* in 1893 had a gross tonnage of 10,498 and a length of 560 feet, while the *Adriatic* had a gross tonnage of 24,541 and a length of 726 feet.

The need for more quay space was obvious, so construction of another dock was immediately commenced and was completed in 1911, being named the White Star Dock, giving additional quays to the length of 3,800 feet together with large single storey transit sheds. After the First World War the Cunard Steamship Company and Canadian Pacific Steamships Ltd., also transferred their express services to the port and this dock was then renamed Ocean Dock.

The commemorative stone which was laid on 12th October 1898 to mark the 60th anniversary of the laying of the Foundation Stone for Southampton Docks. The ceremony was performed by Mr. W.W.B. Beach, M.P., the provincial Grand Master of Freemasons for Hampshire and the Isle of Wight. The location is Dockhead.

Both, Associated British Ports

14

Above: The coal barge jetty at 28 berth on the River Itchen with one of the Cory's colliers alongside discharging coal into barges. Four electrically operated cranes, each capable of lifting five tons with a radius of 52 feet, were provided and these enabled the colliers to be quickly unloaded. The demand for coal gradually decreased, for by the 1930s the majority of the liners used oil fuel instead of coal.

Associated British Ports

Below: The dirty job of coaling a liner – such work continued until the 1930s. The Union Castle ships usually took on about 2,000 tons, but the larger liners, such as the *Olympic*, before they were converted to burn oil fuel, took as much as 4,000 tons. This quantity was normally loaded within twenty hours.

Author's Collection

Left: Advertisements by the London & South Western Railway Company in 1900 concerning Southampton Docks and the steamer services to the Channel Islands and France.

Author's Collection

COALING LINER IN SOUTHAMPTON DOCK

Above: Unloading a cargo of New Zealand fruit from Shaw Savill's motor ship *Taranaki* on to the top floor of the Cold Store at 40 berth in July 1930.

One of the many Elwell-Parker electric trucks used in the port for many years. This one, fully loaded, was taken outside 'C' warehouse in 1934.   *Both, Associated British Ports courtesy Southampton City Museums*

One of the major items of cargo from the Channel Islands – tomatoes – being unloaded in the Outer Dock from the Southern Railway's cargo vessel *Fratton* in June 1931.

Associated British Ports courtesy Southampton City Museums

Years of Expansion

Upon the outbreak of the First World War in August 1914, Southampton was immediately placed under the control of the Government. The port became No. 1 Military Embarkation Port. Except for reduced cross channel services run by the L&SWR from the Outer Dock, all normal traffic ceased. During the course of the war over 7 million officers and men were embarked and disembarked, and more than 3,750,000 tons of stores handled. Sometimes between 25 and 30 ships left the docks in a single night. The despatch of the First Expeditionary Force to France in the early days of the war had been described as one of the greatest achievements of its kind in military history.

In the early 1920s there was an urgent need for additional drydock facilities to accommodate the various large liners which were then based at Southampton, so an order was placed with Armstrong Whitworth & Company for a huge floating drydock, capable of lifting vessels up to 60,000 tons. It was constructed on the Tyne and towed to Southampton. It was officially inaugurated on 27th June 1924 by HRH The Prince of Wales (later to be King Edward VIII and the Duke of Windsor). For the next ten years the great liners then using the port and requiring repair were accommodated in this dock.

In 1923 the grouping of all the important railways in the United Kingdom took place and the London & South Western Railway became part of the Southern Railway Company and so placing control of the docks to the new organisation.

In 1925 the P & O S N Company renewed their association with the port by sending their vessels to the docks on the Far East service.

Thoughts were soon being given to the construction of more docks. In fact prior to the 1914-18 war a large area of land on the Weston Shore side of the River Itchen had been acquired by the railway company with the intention of providing additional docks there, but after the war (in 1923) other plans were developed and the Southern Railway Company obtained parliamentary sanction to initiate the most ambitious scheme of dock extension ever contemplated in the history of the port. The scheme involved the provision, at a cost of £10 million, of a self contained docks estate with 7,000 feet of deep water quays, a 1,200 feet long graving dock and dock equipment requisite for the handling of traffic, including sheds and railway sidings. This formed the Western Docks of today. Progress on the construction of the new quay from just west of the Royal Pier to Millbrook proceeded

17

Left and above: A scene which always proved of interest to Sotonians and visitors alike. From the Town Quay one could often see the spectacle of a large liner in the huge floating dock – on this occasion the *Olympic* – taken on 25th May 1934. The Floating Dock was built on the Tyne and arrived in Southampton in 1924. It had an overall length of 960 feet and a clear width of 134 feet, the height of the side walls being 70 feet. It was necessary to keep its berth dredged to a depth of 65 feet and occasionally the dock was moved to enable this work to be carried out. When this was done in 1932 the dock was berthed alongside the then newly completed part of the quay at 101 berth (above). The dock was there from 23rd May until the 8th July 1932. Eight tugs were involved in moving it. 1934 was the last year that the dock was regularly in use at Southampton. In 1940 it was moved to Portsmouth, being used by the Admiralty as AFD No. 11. In 1959 it was acquired by the Rotterdam Drydock Company and remained in use at Rotterdam until 1983, when that company went out of business. It was sold to owners in Brazil, but was wrecked off the Spanish coast while being towed. *Associated British Ports courtesy Southampton City Museums*

The early 1930s and the New Docks under construction. A start has been made on the storm water pump house, which still remains today. In the foreground is the construction yard which now forms part of Mayflower Park. *Associated British Ports courtesy Southampton City Museums*

Above: The New Docks – early in 1932. Some of the sheds are partly built while James Dredging Company's *Foremost Chief* is pumping dredged material ashore in connection with the reclamation of land which eventually formed part of the Docks Estate.
Associated British Ports

Left: 1932. In the foreground the construction site for the New (Western) Docks which later became Mayflower Park. Alongside the Royal Pier are the paddlers *Queen, Bournemouth Queen* and *Solent Queen*. In the background to the right the Floating Dock towers above the Town Quay and beyond that there are the four funnelled *Mauretania* and the three funnelled *Majestic*.
Associated British Ports

Above: Union Castle's *Rothesay Castle* discharging South African citrus fruit at 101 berth on 27th August 1936. The *Rothesay Castle,* one of the group of Union Castle refrigerated cargo ships built during the 1930s, had a short life for she was wrecked in January 1940.

Right: First shipment of pineapples from the Azores arrives at berth 47 off the *Goncalo Velho* on 29th November 1937.
   Both, Associated British Ports courtesy Southampton City Museums

The huge floating crane, brought into use in 1925, was used for many heavy lifting jobs around the port. It had a maximum lifting capacity of 150 tons. Here it is shown performing one of its more unusual jobs – taking railway rolling stock to the Isle of Wight in the 1930s. The crane was non-propelled – hence the tugs in attendance, but it was fitted with steam machinery in order to perform the lifting operations. In 1962 the steam machinery was replaced by diesel operated equipment. In 1985 it was replaced by a new floating crane which has a lifting capacity of 200 tonnes.

Associated British Ports courtesy Southampton City Museums

King George V drydock at the Millbrook end of the New (Western) Docks under construction during 1932. One of the contractors' locomotives is working on the floor of the dock. The dock is 1,200 feet in length with a width at the entrance of 135 feet. In its construction some 2 million tons of earth were removed and about three quarters of a million tons of concrete were used. The dock has a capacity of 58,000,000 gallons of water at high spring tides. The water can be pumped out in about four hours by four centrifugal type pumps.

Associated British Ports courtesy Southampton City Museums

Above and top right: The opening of No. 7 Drydock – 26th July 1933 – their Majesties King George V and Queen Mary together with the Duke and Duchess of York arrived in the Royal Yacht *Victoria & Albert* and were accompanied to the Dias constructed at the head of the dock for the opening ceremony by Mr. G.W.E. Loder, Chairman of the Southern Railway (left) and Sir Herbert Walker, General Manager of the Southern Railway (right). The yacht severed a red, white and blue ribbon across the entrance upon arrival. Replying to an address of welcome His Majesty recalled that he had accompanied his father to Southampton when he had opened the Prince of Wales' Dock (No. 5 drydock) on 3rd August 1895. The King expressed his admiration for the enterprise displayed by the Board of the Southern Railway in undertaking the work of building the dock and said 'I have pleasure in declaring the dock open for use and in naming it 'The King George V Graving Dock' and I pray that by God's blessing it may serve to foster and increase the commerce of Southampton'. When the King had finished speaking, Mr. Loder passed a silver cup filled with wine to the Queen and Her Majesty, leaning over the balustrade, poured the wine into the flower edged water. The opening ceremony was followed by a short religious service conducted by the Lord Bishop of Winchester after which the Royal Party embarked in the Royal Yacht and returned to Cowes. *Southampton City Museums*

Right: The first liner to use the drydock was the White Star Line's *Majestic* shown here entering the drydock on the 19th January 1934. The *Majestic* was then the largest ship in the world, entering the then largest drydock in the world. It will be seen on the right the land for the dock estate has still to be reclaimed.
Author's Collection

The ground floor effect – work being carried out to the propellers of the *Majestic* in King George V drydock during the 1930s.

Associated British Ports courtesy Southampton City Museums

A superb view of the four funnelled *Mauretania* being manoeuvred by a fleet of tugs on 19th October 1932 when the liner became the first ship to be berthed alongside the New (Western) Docks.

Associated British Ports

The docks during the morning of 29th June 1935. Cunard White Star Line's *Ausonia* is just arriving – heading for the vacant berth 47 in the Ocean Dock. Other ships in that dock are *Arandora Star* at 46 berth, *Voltaire* at 44 and the *Georgic* at 43 berth. The *Essequibo* is in No. 6 drydock – that vessel had been sold to the Russians and was undergoing repair. Alongside the Cold Store at 40 berth is Shaw Savill's *Mataroa*, no doubt discharging produce from New Zealand. The four funnelled *Arundel Castle* is in No. 5 drydock, while in the Empress Dock is the troopship *Neuralia* and the banana carrier *Erin*. On the Itchen Quays are the two funnelled *Alcantara* and Ellerman Lines *City of Nagpur*, which at the time was carrying out a series of cruises from the port. In the New Docks are Orient Line's *Orama* at 101 berth, North German Lloyd's *Bremen*, P&O *Moldavia* and the four funnellers *Mauretania* and *Olympic*. Two days after this photograph was taken the *Mauretania* sailed to Rosyth to be broken up.

Associated British Ports courtesy Southampton City Museums

quickly and on the 19th October 1932 the first ship to berth at the new quay was the Cunard four-funnelled *Mauretania*. The channel giving access to the new quay was dredged to a minimum depth of 35 feet at low water (spring tides) and was made at least 600 feet wide. A total area of about 400 acres was reclaimed from the sea and the majority of the land was incorporated into the docks estate. The first factory to be constructed on the site was Ranks Mill which opened in 1934 and still remains in operation today.

At the Millbrook end of the new quay the new graving dock was constructed and involved the excavation of about two million tons of earth. About 750,000 tons of concrete was used in the construction of the walls and floor. On 26th July 1933 the dock was officially named 'King George V drydock' by HM King George V accompanied by HM Queen Mary who arrived in the royal yacht *Victoria & Albert*. When completed, the drydock was the largest in the world; it has a length of 1,200 feet, the width at the entrance is 135 feet, and it can be pumped dry within four hours. Cunard White Star's *Majestic* was the first liner to use the drydock in January 1934; it was here that the *Queen Mary* was placed when she first arrived in the port from her builders on 27th March 1936.

In 1935 there was an important addition to the ships operating from the port, when the French Line (Compagnie Generale Transatlantique) substituted Southampton for Plymouth as a port of call for their liners engaged on the North Atlantic and West Indies services. The popularity of cruising also brought in more ships and passengers. In 1928 there were 18,000 cruising passengers passing through the port, with by 1936 the number rising to 70,000.

With so many of the large and popular liners using the port many sightseers were attracted to Southampton and by 1939 there were as many as 500,000 each year, many of them travelling by special excursions offered by the Southern Railway's trains and steamers.

In 1934 Imperial Airways decided to use the flying boats instead of land planes on its Empire route to South Africa, by the way of the Mediterranean, Nile and East African coast to Durban, also on the route to India, the Far East and Australia. A large number of four engined flying-boats were built for the services. The first all-air services began by flying boat from Southampton to Alexandria in 1937, and in the same year this service was extended to South Africa. Experimental flights were made across the North Atlantic, preparatory to the inauguration of regular services; the Empire Air Mail programme was extended, bringing India within three days of England, Singapore five and half days and South Africa five days.

Above: The Inner Dock in April 1937 showing one of the massive quayside warehouses. The steamer is the Great Western Railway's *Sambur* under repair by J.I. Thornycroft's men. In the foreground is the small *Moultonian*, which plied for many years between Southampton, mainly from the Town Quay to the Isle of Wight.

Left: Unloading a cargo of cotton seed from the Greek steamer *Filomila* at 26 berth in the Empress Dock on 12th June 1934. In the background several banana vans can be seen at 24/5 berths, where Fyffes bananas were regularly unloaded.
Both, Associated British Ports courtesy Southampton City Museums

Above: The export of vehicles has been an important feature of the trade through the port for many years – here is part of a shipment of 200 Fordson tractors for the American market, which were loaded on to Bernstein Line's *Pennland* at 106 berth on 29th January 1937.

Right: Timber being unloaded from the steamer *Leyland* at 45 berth at the north end of the Ocean Dock, showing the specially constructed shed for timber traffic erected in the early 1920s. Two of Alexandra Towing Company's tugs can be seen – the *William Poulsom* and the *Gladstone*.
Both, Associated British Ports courtesy Southampton City Museums

Canadian Pacific Steamship's *Duchess of Richmond* undergoing annual refit in No. 6 Trafalgar drydock in January 1938. This vessel survived the war and in 1947 was renamed *Empress of Canada*, being burnt out at Liverpool in January 1953.

Associated British Ports courtesy Southampton City Museums

Above: The administration of the docks was carried out from this building from 1872 until the present Dock Office was opened at the end of 1962. The building was later used by Townsend Thoresen Car Ferries, until they moved to Portsmouth. The decoration on this occasion was for the Coronation of King George VI in May 1937.

Right: Unveiling the 100th anniversary memorial near No. 8 gate in the Western Docks. The ceremony was performed on the 12th October 1938 by the then chairman of the Southern Railway, Mr. Robert Holland-Martin. For one hour from noon to 1 pm the bells of St. Marys and Holy Rood Churches joyously pealed forth to mark the occasion. The column is 8 feet 6 inches high and is surmounted by a bronze globe girdled by an equitoral band bearing the signs of the Zodiac. After the ceremony, lunch for about 330 special guests was provided on board Royal Mail Lines' *Austrias.*

    Both, Associated British Ports courtesy Southampton City Museums

At one time the flying boats operated from a pontoon off 101 berth, but in 1938 moved to 108 berth, served by the new purpose-built Imperial House. With the outbreak of war in September 1939 the air services were abandoned, but later in the war were partly revived, operating from Poole Harbour.

On the 12th October 1938, the then chairman of the Southern Railway, Robert Holland-Martin, unveiled the Centenary Memorial on the same date as the laying of the foundation stone one hundred years earlier. The bronze globe is now located outside Ocean Gate, the new Dock Office.

The Ocean Dock in July/ August 1939. The *Queen Mary* is on the right and the new *Mauretania* at 46 berth on the left. Between the two liners at 45 berth is a small timber ship discharging timber into railway wagons.
Associated British Ports

The New Docks fifty years ago – 29th June 1938. The *Queen Mary* is in No. 7 drydock undergoing her summer overhaul and alongside the quays are the three funnelled *Berengaria* (then laid up), *Marie Bakke* (discharging timber from the Baltic), P&O's *Strathallan* and *Stratheden*, Orient's *Orford*, P&O's *Viceroy of India* and the United States Lines' *Manhattan*. In the Old Docks are Union Castle's *Balmoral Castle* at 38 berth, *Windsor Castle* and *Alcantara* on the Itchen Quays.

Southampton City Museums

World War Two Effort

No one could have dreamt that within a few years of the completion of the new docks they would take on a completely new role. The days just before the outbreak of the Second World War on 3rd September 1939 saw a build up of troops and equipment in the docks and this continued during the following months. The passenger liners left for less vulnerable bases, many of them being converted to armed merchant cruisers or troopships. Early in 1940 the large floating dock was moved to Portsmouth having been acquired by the Admiralty. The events of 1940 completely changed the situation. The port's role as a supply bridge-head for the British Expeditionary Force altered with the collapse of France. With the over-running of the French Channel and Atlantic coasts Southampton became more vulnerable to attack, and in view of a threatened invasion the port was closed to all but coastal ships. Repair of damaged and mined vessels continued to flourish in the company's and other repair yards.

The air attacks in the summer of 1940 and the blitz of the winter of 1940/41 left their marks on the docks with considerable damage to buildings (including the Cold Store at berth 40), but the quays, drydocks and equipment escaped lightly. In 1942 the port was re-opened for 'leaselend' cargoes of much needed foodstuffs and essential war materials from America.

Early in 1943 preparations began for the invasion of France. Much of the famous Mulberry Harbour, to be floated across the Channel, was constructed in the dock area. Before 'D' day (6th June 1944) troops and equipment were loaded onto landing craft which left for anchorages in Southampton Water prior to crossing the Channel. A train ferry terminal was established to the west of King George V drydock to replenish the French railways.

During the war years there was a total of 69 air-raids affecting the docks, resulting in 23 transit sheds or warehouses being destroyed, while many others were damaged although later repaired. 4.3 million troops passed through the port together with 3.9 million tons of stores and equipment.

The International Cold Store at 40 berth on the Test Quays on fire after being damaged during an air-raid in August 1940. The contents, much of it butter, smouldered for two or three weeks.

Author's Collection

Air raid damage. The remains of 'M' warehouse, Inner Dock, after raids on 30th November and 2nd December 1940.

Author's Collection

The scene in June 1944. Rows and rows of Landing Craft alongside the New Docks – ready for the 'D' Day invasion of Europe.

Author's Collection

Many strange looking craft were to be seen in the Southampton area during the build-up to 'D' Day, here is a section of the Mulberry Harbour being moved in May 1944.

Author's Collection

Above: The *Queen Mary*, still in her wartime livery, returns to Southampton on 11th August 1945, the first time for six years.

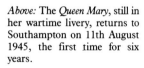

Right: Sir Winston Churchill arriving at the docks on 18th March 1949 to embark on the *Queen Elizabeth*. He is here seen shaking hands with Sir Reginald Biddle, then Docks & Marine Manager. Winston Churchill had made various visits to the docks during the war years to see for himself the volume of traffic being handled in the war effort.

Both, Associated British Ports

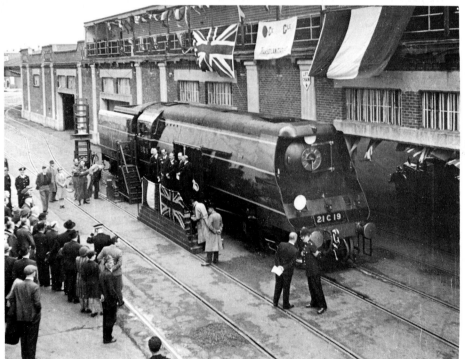

Above: In April 1946 a Southern Railway boat train leaves 44 Shed behind 'King Arthur' class No. 739 *King Leodegrance* – the *Queen Mary* is still in her wartime grey.

Left: During the 1940s the Southern Railway constructed a class of thirty 4-6-2 main line locomotives and these were all named after shipping companies, many of them having connections with the port. On 22nd September 1945 a special ceremony was held at 104 berth for the naming of *French Line – CGT.* Many distinguished personalities were present and alongside the quay was the liner *Ile de France* which was being officially handed back to her French owners after war service.

Both, Associated British Ports

By the middle of 1947 the sheds at 43/4 berths had been demolished in preparation for the construction·of the Ocean Terminal. The vessel alongside at 44 berth is the troop transport *El Nil*.

Associated British Ports

Post War Development

The end of the war in 1945 heralded the return of several of the well known liners to the port, including the *Queen Mary* on the 11th August 1945, while on the 20th August 1945 the *Queen Elizabeth* arrived in the port for the first time. The latter sailed on her maiden passage commercial voyage from Southampton on 16th October 1946 with the *Queen Mary* returning to full commercial service on 31st July 1947.

By then changes in administration were in progress, for nationalisation of various transport undertakings, including the railways, was brought about by the Transport Act of 1947, which saw the establishment of the British Transport Commission. This body assumed control of the docks as from 1st January 1948. On 1st September 1950 the control of the docks passed to the Docks & Inland Waterways Executive. The Transport Act of 1953 brought about further changes resulting in the docks being separated from the Inland Waterways and the establishment of the British Transport Docks Division directly responsible to the British Transport Commission.

Imperial Airways became part of British Overseas Airways Corporation in 1940, and they returned to Southampton after the war and a new terminal at 50 berth was opened on 14th April 1948 by Lord Nathan. BOAC replaced their flying boats with land planes in 1950 and left the port, but Aquila Airways took over until 1958 when they too ceased operations. In 1963 the building was taken over by HMS Wessex, the Solent Division of the RNR.

In 1946 a decision was made to replace the two single storey sheds at 43/44 berths with an Ocean Terminal worthy of the country's premier passenger port. Demolition of the old sheds was commenced in December 1946 and the new building completed in 1950, being officially opened by the then Prime Minister, the Rt.Hon. C.R. Atlee on 31st July, 1950. The following day the Terminal was used for the first time for the sailing of Cunard's *Queen Elizabeth*. The 8th July 1952 saw the arrival at the Terminal of the new liner *United States* on completion of her maiden voyage. (With the decline in the number of passengers ships using the port, the building was taken out of use at the end of 1980 being eventually demolished in 1983.)

During the war the Transit Shed at 102 berth in the Western Docks was severely damaged and in 1952 it was decided to

Above: The Marine Air Terminal at 50 berth shortly after completion in 1948 for the BOAC flying boat services. The building remains in use today by HMS Wessex, the Solent Division of the RNR. No. 6 (Trafalgar) drydock is not occupied but at the head of the dock can be seen the 'V' section cut into it in 1922 to permit the *Berengaria* to use it. This photograph also clearly shows the extent of Harland & Wolff's workshops. The workshops were demolished in 1987 in conjunction with various proposed non-operational developments which have been delayed owing to the present recession.

Left: BOAC's Short S45 Solent flying boat *Southampton* alongside the Marine Air Terminal at 50 berth. This aircraft was named *Southampton* on 14th April 1948 by the Mayoress of Southampton at the inauguration of the then new Terminal. *Both, Associated British Ports Courtesy Southampton City Museums*

June 1950 and the Ocean Terminal is practically completed. It was opened by the Prime Minister, the Rt. Hon. C.R. Atlee on 31st July 1950. The *Queen Elizabeth* is at 46/7 berths, while in the Empress Dock is the emigrant carrier *New Australia*, still being fitted out by J.I. Thornycroft & Company, and Fyffes *Matina* with Royal Mail Lines *Andes* on the Itchen Quays. The Ocean Terminal building, which cost £750,000, had a length of 1,297 feet and a width of 111 feet. Its railway platform could deal with two trains simultaneously. A visitors balcony extended the length of the building and at the seaward end a tower housed customs offices, etc. On the upper floor two large passenger lounges were provided, each having a refreshment buffet, telephone kiosks, banking facilities together with various other items required by passengers. Adjacent to the lounges were customs examination halls. Passengers to or from liners embarked or disembarked direct between ship and the lounges by means of 3 sets of two hydraulically operated telescopic gangways fitted to the outside of the building. Heavy baggage from ships was landed to the quay by mechanical baggage conveyors and thence moved to the upper floor by a series of conveyors. One of Red Funnel's paddlers goes astern after allowing passengers a view of the liner and the new building. The building was demolished in 1983.

Associated British Ports courtesy Southampton City Museums

The completed Ocean Terminal with the *Queen Elizabeth* alongside being refuelled by one of the oil refuelling barges. In the background at 45 berth is the troopship *Empire Ken*.

Author's Collection

One of the two luxurious passenger lounges provided on the upper floor of the Ocean Terminal.

Associated British Ports

The Old (Eastern) Docks – 14th June 1949 – showing the layout of the sheds at Dockhead, and also the mass of railway sidings to the rear of these sheds. The *Queen Mary* is at 46/7 berths and on the opposite side of the Ocean Dock, the Ocean Terminal is under construction with the troopship *Empire Windrush* at 44 berth. Another troopship, the *Eastern Prince*, is at 40 berth and ahead of her at 38/9 berths is the *Capetown Castle*, ready for the next outward sailing to the Cape. On the Itchen Quays are the *Arundel Castle*, *Dunera* and *Andes*. In the Empress Dock is the troopship *Empire Orwell* refitting and to the right of this vessel is the *El Nil*. Two railway-owned cargo vessels – the *Ringwood* and *Haslemere* are also in the Empress Dock while in the Outer Dock is the *Falaise* and the *Isle of Guernsey*. The Dover-based train ferry *Hampton Ferry* is in No. 5 drydock.
Associated British Ports courtesy Southampton City Museums

construct a new two-storey terminal for the Union Castle's mail service to South Africa. This building was officially opened on 25th January 1956 by the High Commissioner for South Africa, Mr G.P. Jooste. Union Castle's *Edinburgh Castle* was the first ship to use the new facilities. The building remains, at present, forming part of the Free Trade Zone.

For many years two of the major items of import cargo arriving in the ships of the Union Castle Line were wool and fruit. During the 1950s and 1960s over a quarter of a million bales of wool each year were shipped through the port, while the fruit, both citrus and deciduous, amounted to millions of packages annually.

In 1954 Standard Telephone & Cables Ltd acquired a site in the New (Western) Docks with the intention of constructing a large factory for the manufacture of submarine telephone cable. The first shipment of cable made in the factory was loaded in November 1956 by means of an overhead gantry direct from the factory to a cable ship at 109 berth.

On 9th August 1956 the Royal yacht *Britannia* called on the first of several occasions to embark Her Majesty the Queen and other members of the Royal Family. During the same year the Trafalgar drydock was modernised with the provision of stabiliser recesses in the sides and the electrification of the caisson machinery.

The year 1956 also saw the commencement of the construction of a new Cold Store for the International Cold Store and Ice Company at 108 berth and this was brought into use on 16th July 1958, with the arrival of the *Brisbane Star* from New Zealand. The building remained in use until June 1981, when it was closed due to a dramatic decrease in the demand for cold storage facilities in ports following the refrigeration of cargoes in containers.

On 17th January 1958 the Southampton Harbour Board inaugurated a Port Operations and Information Service based at Calshot, with harbour surveillance and a comprehensive VHF radio-telephone communication system. It was the first of its kind in the world. During the same year improved passenger facilities were provided in the shed at No. 31 berth on the River Itchen to serve passenger ships using berth 30-33.

During 1959 the reconstruction of the pre-war pas-

Above: July 1949. The three drydocks, entrance for which was obtained from the Outer Dock. On the right, No. 1 drydock, the first to be opened in 1846, the centre one, No. 2 was opened in the following year, and No. 3, on the left, was brought into use in 1854. At the top end of No. 2 drydock is the pumping station and beyond that the engine sheds for the docks shunting engines. On the Itchen Quays are Royal Mail Lines' *Alcantara* and British Railways train ferry *Hampton Ferry* from Dover for overhaul. On the left of the picture part of No. 4 drydock, opened in 1879, can be seen. In the background are two of the oil re-fuelling barges alongside the Jetty from the Weston shore.

Left: Stag Line's *Begonia* alongside 102/3 berths in the 1950s – this shows one of the two electrically operated travelling intake plants. Each plant was fitted with two suction pipes which sucked up the grain from the ship's holds and transferred it to conveyor belts direct to Rank's Mill, some 600 feet away. Each plant was capable of dealing with 120 tons of grain per hour.
Both, Associated British Ports courtesy Southampton City Museums

Above: The two storey building constructed at 102 berth in the Western Docks, and brought into use in 1956 for dealing with the weekly arrivals of Union Castle mail ships from South Africa - the *Edinburgh Castle* is alongside. The building was 932 feet in length and had a width of 108 feet. The upper storey was used for handling cargo, particularly wool. Behind the building (top left) can be seen the numerous railway sidings which existed leading to the large carriage cleaning shed which has been demolished. Also to be seen is Rank's Solent Flour Mills and the two enclosed conveyor belts for grain leading direct from the quayside to the Mills. *Below:* The interior of the Waiting Hall at 102. *Author's Collection*

Passengers embarking on Union Castle Line's *Edinburgh Castle* on Thursday 7th October 1954. No doubt the vessel sailed at 4.00pm as usual.

Associated British Ports courtesy Southampton City Museums

The Outer Dock in the 1950s with British Railways steamers *Brittany, Isle of Guernsey* and *Falaise.*

Associated British Ports

Above: The liner *United States,* having sailed from the New (Western) Docks, passes the Old (Eastern) Docks in April 1959. At 46 berth in the Ocean Dock is the *Mauretania* with the troopship *Oxfordshire* astern, while in No. 6 (Trafalgar) drydock is Home Lines' *Homeric.* On the right can be seen the works of Harland & Wolff Ltd.
Southampton City Museums

Right: The all Pullman car boat train 'Statesman' alongside the Ocean Terminal on 8th July 1952 in connection with the arrival of the liner *United States* after her record breaking maiden voyage across the Atlantic. The locomotive at the head of the train is 'West Country' class No. 34007 *Wadebridge* with the appropriate headboard.
M. Beckett Collection

senger waiting hall between 105/6 berths was commenced and the new accommodation was officially opened on 29th November 1960 by Field Marshal, the Rt. Hon. Viscount Slim. It was used for the first time on 3rd December by Orient Line's *Oriana* for her maiden voyage to Australia. This terminal has recently been modernised and is now known as the Mayflower Cruise Terminal, used mainly by passengers travelling on P&O cruise ships, *Victoria, Oriana* and the *Arcadia* which has replaced the *Canberra.* ABP has recently signed a four-year contract with P&O Cruises for Southampton to be their exclusive UK base through into the Millennium.

During the early 1960s several new passenger liners

entered service, such as *Oriana, Canberra,* the *France, Windsor Castle* and *Transvaal Castle* (renamed *SA Vaal* in 1966), but they would increasingly turn their trade into full-time cruising rather than the regular passenger services they were built for.

In January 1960 new banana discharge facilities were brought into use at Berths 24/5 in the Empress Dock for Fyffes traffic. The equipment included four shore based telescopic gantry conveyors with continuous conveyor belts for loading units both road and rail. In the following year a small passenger waiting hall was added to cater for those passenger travelling by the banana ships.

The transit sheds at 26/7 berths in the Empress Docks

Bananas being unloaded at 24/5 berths from one of Fyffes' ships, *Changuinola*, in January 1960 when these four overhead gantries were brought into use. Endless chains with canvas pockets were lowered into the hold and the canvas pockets carried the stems of bananas into the shed where they were tipped on to a horizontal belt (left) and moved to the loading point for stowing into railway vans or road vehicles. Some 14,000 stems of bananas per hour could be discharged with this equipment. In later years the bananas arrived in cardboard cartons.

Associated British Ports

Although the Eastern Docks is well full of ships, this was for rather a sad occasion – the British Seamen's Strike in June 1966. The *Queen Mary* is at the Ocean Terminal and astern of her are two Union Castle 'R' class ships – *Roxburgh Castle* and *Rowallan Castle*. At 46 berth is Cunard's *Carmania* with Port Line's *Port Lyttleton* alongside and at 47 berth is P&O *Arcadia*, while Royal Mail Lines' *Andes* is in No. 6 (Trafalgar) drydock and Fyffes *Camito* and *Golfito* are off 50 berth. *Associated British Ports courtesy Southampton City Museums*

were destroyed by enemy action during the war and so in 1961 a new cargo shed, designed mainly for fruit cargoes, was brought into use. The outside platform was served by a flush fitted rail track to enable it to be used by rail or road vehicles.

In 1961 British Railways decided that their passenger services to the Channel Islands would be operated entirely from Weymouth, and so the Southampton–Channel Islands passenger service came to an end with the arrival of the *Isle of Guernsey* on 12th May 1961. Three years later, on 9th May 1964, the Le Havre service was withdrawn and on 27th September the St. Malo service was closed down, thus ending all British Railways' passengers sailings from the port. The cargo service to the Channel Islands remained until 1972 when it was transferred to Portsmouth.

In 1962 the Rochdale Committee, set up by the Government to investigate future policy options for the country's commercial ports, reported that Southampton's natural facilities and land availability and inland connections made it eminently suitable for development to meet modern trends in shipping.

From 1872 the administration of the docks had been carried out from the building adjacent to the then No. 7 Gate (now the entrance to the Ocean Village), but in December 1962 a five-storey office block was brought into use. The Transport Act of 1962 abolished the British Transport Commission so as from the 1st January 1963 the British Transport Dock Board became an independent statutory authority. A major change in the administration of the whole port area occurred on 1st August 1968 when the Southampton Harbour Board was amalgamated with the British Transport Docks Board. The BTDB assumed full responsibility for the administration and conservancy of the whole port area including Fawley and the Town Quay in addition to the Docks.

July 1972 saw the opening of the new port signal and Radar station at Dockhead, replacing the one based at Calshot. For the first time in the history of the port all maritime activities were centred into one building, including the Dock & Harbour Master's offices, Operations Room and Trinity House pilots. The station radar and VHF covers the whole of the port area to the Nab Tower in the eastern Solent and to the entrance in the western Solent.

The Outer Dock, which was renamed Princess Alexandra Dock in 1967. Swedish Lloyd's *Patricia*, which is on the berth on the right, entered service between Southampton and Bilbao in the spring of 1967. Work is still being carried out on berth 2 which was first used by Southern Ferries (later to become P&O Ferries) during the summer of 1967 for their Le Havre service. In the foreground, the majority of which was originally the Inner Dock, work is progressing to develop the area for parking of vehicles and cars etc awaiting shipment. The whole of this area now forms Ocean Village. The building with the curved roof just to the left of the *Patricia* was the Passenger Terminal for these ferries.

Associated British Ports courtesy Southampton City Museums

The link span installed at No. 6 berth in the Outer Dock for Thoresens car ferry services which commenced operations in 1964.

Associated British Ports

The passenger/cargo terminal at 38/9 berths when new in June 1966 – the building was officially opened by Her Majesty The Queen during the following month. The terminal is 930 feet in length and passenger accommodation is provided on the first floor of the centrally located double storeyed section. The vessel alongside is Union Castle's *Pendennis Castle*, while in No. 5 drydock (top left) is Fyffes *Chicanoa*. With the exception of the Terminal, all the sheds in the photograph have been demolished and No. 5 drydock has been filled in. Part of the area is now occupied by grain storage silos operated by Southampton Grain Silo Ltd while the rest of the area is used for the storage of cars and vehicles.

Associated British Ports courtesy Southampton City Museums

Developments in Recent Years

In February 1963 the Inner Dock, first used in 1851, was closed and subsequently filled in. The area of land reclaimed with the filling in was used for storage and for cars awaiting shipment. The first of the cross channel car ferry services was commenced in May 1964 by the Norwegian Thoresen Car Ferries. For this service a passenger waiting hall was provided at 6 Berth and a link-span installed parallel with 7 Berth, while sheds 7/8 were modified for the handling of cars and passengers disembarking. During the following years several more ferry services were attracted to the Port. Additional facilities were provided at 2/3 Berths, including a new waiting hall which was opened on 3rd July 1967, when the Outer Dock was renamed Princess Alexandra Dock. On 5th April 1967 Swedish Lloyd's *Patricia* made her first sailing to Bilbao, and on 29th June 1967 Southern Ferries (later to become Normandy Ferries and P&O Ferries) started their service to Le Havre with the sailing of the

Dragon. Two years later they extended their services to Lisbon and Casablanca with the larger *Eagle*. In 1965 another link-span for roll-on/roll-off traffic became operational at 49 Berth. Unfortunately several of the ferry services were rather short-lived, although Swedish Lloyd's service to Spain lasted until 1977, while Townsend Thoresen Ferries transferred all their services to Portsmouth by 1983. The following year, P&O Ferries also moved their operations to Portsmouth.

There was then a gap in Cross Channel services from the Port until 1991, when Stena Sealink Line decided to introduce the ferry *Stena Normandy* on a regular service to Cherbourg. A new passenger terminal was provided at 30 Berth. The service proved very popular and during 1992 a total of 508,142 passengers and over 90,000 cars were carried in addition to freight traffic. However, in 1996 the traffic declined due to the introduction of the Channel Tunnel and the service was withdrawn.

Western Docks in 1970. Right to left are S.A. *Vaal* (formerly the *Transvaal Castle*); the former troopship *Nevasa*, then in use as a 'School' ship being refuelled by an Esso tanker; P&O *Iberia*,

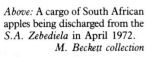

Above: A cargo of South African apples being discharged from the *S.A. Zebediela* in April 1972.
M. Beckett collection

Right: Four of the principal types of locomotives which have served Southampton Docks over the years. Left to right – Adams 'B4', the American 0-6-0T, LB & SCR 0-6-0T and one of the Ruston Hornsby diesel electric shunters. In the background is the liner *Canberra* in No. 7 drydock. *The late G. Wheeler*

51

The floating crane being overhauled in No. 7 drydock in 1979. This view shows the massive area of the dock which is today used by A&P Appledore Ltd.

R. Mursell collection

Above: Plenty of activity when Cunard's *Queen Elizabeth 2* arrives in the Port. The liner was extensively refitted in 1995 and now carries a new dark blue livery on her hull.

Right: Red Eagle, one of the ferries operated by Red Funnel Group which provides high-speed passenger/freight services to Cowes on the Isle of Wight. The Red Funnel Group is now owned by ABP Holdings Plc.   *Both, Associated British Ports*

On the 15th July 1966 HM The Queen and Prince Philip opened the new passenger/cargo terminal at 38/39 Berths. Royal consent was given soon afterwards to name the building 'Queen Elizabeth II Terminal'. It was designed for dealing with cargo on the ground floor, an area of 928 feet in length and 165 feet wide, making it available for uninterrupted operations. The passenger accommodation is on the first floor in the centre of the terminal. The building was modernised during 1995 increasing the space dedicated to passenger handling operations. It is one of two modern deep-sea passenger terminals in the Port.

During the early 1960s time was beginning to run out for the passenger liners using the Port with most transatlantic travellers preferring to use the speedier services of jet aircraft. Perhaps the most well-know of liners, the *Queen Mary*, completed her last North Atlantic crossing at the end of September 1967 and sailed from the Port for the last time on 31st October for Long Beach, California. She remains there as a hotel, conference and tourist attraction.

In November of the following year, the *Queen Elizabeth* made her final departure from Southampton. After a spell in the USA she was moved to Hong Kong and whilst being refitted was gutted by fire in January 1972. By now the

QE2 had been launched and would make her maiden voyage from Southampton to New York on 2nd May 1969. In November of 1969, the *United States* was withdrawn from service and laid up. The French Line decided to withdraw their *France* in September 1974, but that vessel was reprieved and is now operating as the *Norway*, sometimes calling into Southampton once again. The end of an era occurred on 16th September 1977 when

Southampton Container Terminals

SHENZHEN BAY
LONDON

Above: The Gateway, or road entrance to the Container Terminal in the Western Docks.

Left: P&O Containers' Shenzhen Bay was the first ship to use the new 207 Berth.

Below: The 66,086 GRT *OOCL Netherlands* made her maiden voyage to Southampton Container Terminals in January 1998.

All photos, Associated British Ports

the *Southampton Castle* left Southampton on the last sailing of the Union Castle mail service to South Africa - a service which had commenced in 1857.

April 1982 saw troops passing through the Port again when the liners *Canberra* and *QE2* were requisitioned for the Falklands campaign. Fortunately both ships returned to Southampton and re-entered passenger service later in the year. Security in the Port has always been of paramount importance and as early as 1839 two watchmen were employed wearing police uniform and undoubtedly were the forerunners of the Dock Police force which existed for many years. In 1985 the Police were replaced by a security company.

In 1981 the two remaining drydocks, Numbers 6 and 7, were leased to British Shipbuilders - later to become Vosper Shiprepairers. When this company failed, the lease was taken on by Thew Engineering. In 1989 No.6 drydock was taken out of use. Thew Engineering left No. 7 drydock in 1990 when A & P Southampton Ltd took over.

Containerisation

Whilst primarily a passenger port, the amount of cargo handled through Southampton has been considerable; during the early 1900s it passed the one million ton mark and that figure was regularly maintained during the 1920s and 1930s. The figures for the last fifteen years, however,

Early days at the Container berths – December 1969 – only the first berth approximately 900 feet in length was then complete. The vessel alongside is one of the Atlantic Container Line's ships *Atlantic Causeway* which made her maiden voyage from Southampton in December 1969.
Associated British Ports

A scene prior to the demolition of the Marchwood Power Station. The white hulled Safmarine *S.A. Waterberg* is at 204 berth and P&O Container's *Cardigan Bay* is at 205 berth. The former berths at 201/2 are now full of cars.
Associated British Ports

clearly indicate how the whole nature of operations in the Port have changed - in 1981 the total cargo amounted to 2,095,000 tonnes. In 1987 it reached 6,634,306 tonnes and in 1996 it was 9,526,400 tonnes. Containerisation has played a major part, but there are several other major flows of traffic such as vehicles, grain, bulk wine, animal feed and vegetables and fruit from the Canaries and the West Indies.

In 1965 plans were revealed for a £60 million extension of the New Docks (renamed Western Docks in 1965) with the provision of additional quays between King George V drydock and Redbridge. A parliamentary Bill for this extension received the Royal Assent on 9th August 1966 and on 25th January 1967, the Minister of Transport authorised the first stage of the extension consisting of a berth, about 900 feet in length, together with 20 acres of land for specialised container ship operation. The dredging work commenced in February 1967 and the berth (to become 201) was used for the first time on 27th October 1968 by the *Teniers* of the Belgian Line (later to become part of Dart Container Line). On 4th December 1969 Atlantic Container's *Atlantic Causeway* made her maiden voyage from the Port and soon afterwards Seatrain commenced their operations. The quay was subsequently extended by another 900 feet creating a second berth, number 202.

Towards the end of 1969 it was announced that Overseas Containers (now P&O Containers), Associated Containers and Ben Line, had selected Southampton as their sole United Kingdom port of call for their Far East service due to commence in 1972. Approval was obtained for the provision of additional quays to the length of 3,900 feet to cater for the increase in trade. Work on this extension commenced in June 1970. Soon afterwards the British firms involved were joined by Hapag Lloyd, Nippon Yusen Kaisha and Mitsui OSK Lines to operated a combined service to the Far East under the collective name of 'Trio Lines' with an initial fleet of seventeen vessels. The first ship to call on this service was NYK's *Kamakura Maru* which used 202 Berth on 29th January 1972. Berth 204 was first used on 8th June 1972 with the sailing of OCL's *Tokyo Bay*. Linked with these new container berths was the provision of a Maritime Freightliner terminal,

opened in March 1972. Later, the South Africa Conference Lines decided to use Southampton for their South Africa - Europe container service and Berth 206 was brought into use for this in May 1978.

Since 1986 Berths 201/2 have been used for vehicle traffic. In December 1996 a new 420 metre 207 Berth was brought into use, thereby considerably increasing the terminal quay length - there are now 1350 metres available. During 1997 the equivalent of 892,000 20-foot container units passed through the terminal which is operated by Southampton Container Terminals Ltd., a company jointly owned by ABP and P&O Containers Ltd. Over recent years the Company has invested heavily in providing new equipment - eight new straddle carriers were supplied in 1996 by the Finnish manufacturer SISU Terminal Systems Inc. to work in conjunction with the Valmet machines which can stack one container over two, but the SISU machines can stack one container over three, thereby considerably increasing the capacity of the stacking area. During 1997 three new quayside gantry cranes were brought into use - these cranes have an outreach of 50 metres with a standard lift rating of 40 tonnes, but with a heavy lift capacity up to 66 tonnes. Another important development has been the completion of the main channel dredge which has increased the depth of the approach channel between Fawley and Berth 207 from 10.2 metres to 12.6 metres. This allows the largest loaded container ships to have access to the Port for 18 out of every 24 hours.

In 1992 Trio Lines were disbanded and P&O Containers combined with the Danish Maersk Line to provide a joint service to the Far East, while Hapag Lloyd and the Japanese companies also operated a joint service. In 1996 the services to the Far East were completely revised, resulting in more container vessels calling at Southampton. This was due to the formation of the 'Grand Alliance' involving P&O/Nedlloyd, Hapag Lloyd, Neptune Orient and Nippon Yusen Kaisha (NYK), plus the 'Global Alliance' with Mitsui OSK Lines, Orient Oversea Container Lines, Malaysian International Shipping Corporation and American President Lines. In addition, Maersk Line in conjunction with Sea-Land operated a fast service to and from the Far East.

As from March 1998 various changes in the Alliances occurred - Orient Overseas Containers and Malaysian International joined the Grand Alliance, while the Global Alliance became the 'New World Alliance' formed of Hyundai M Marine, American President Lines/NOL and Mitsui OSK Lines. In addition Maersk Line's fast service to the Far East was transferred from Southampton.

Vehicle Traffic

For many years new cars and vehicles have been passing through Southampton. A major impetus, however, was given to this traffic when the French car manufacturing firm of Renault decided to use Southampton for the importing of their vehicles for the British market. The first shipment of cars arrived in 1960 and this trade still flourishes today. In 1980 a floating link-span was installed at 104/5 Berths in the Western Docks originally for the unloading of Renault cars. This link-span

Left: Cars awaiting export and in the foreground more cars arrive by train.
Associated British Ports

Above: Four vehicle carriers in the Eastern Docks in May 1996 - in the foreground is Wallenius Lines *Faust,* on the left is Wallenius *Lines Madame Butterfly,* then Hual *Sanwa* and NYK's *Jingu Maru.* The grain silos at 36 Berth can be clearly seen and immediately behind them is the QEII terminal. *Below:* Ford Motor Company's new small vehicle, the Ka, arrived in Britain for the first time at Berth 201/2 in October 1996.

Above: The Chinese *Li Shan Hai* (35,842 gross tons) loaded 60,300 tonnes of grain at 47 Berth in September 1995.   *Associated British Ports*
Below: The grain silos at 36 Berth in the Eastern Docks. These are operated by Soufflet Grain Terminal Ltd. and were brought into use in 1983. The Lithuanian *Kapitonas Panfilov* is alongside being loaded.   *M. Beckett*

can now be used by all types of vehicles and is used for freight roll-on/roll-off traffic to and from the Continent. The movement of road vehicles through the Port is not just in one direction, for since the early 1970s the import and export of cars and other vehicles has steadily increased. In December 1976 a link-span was brought into operation at 30 Berth on the Itchen Quays, while in 1988 an additional high capacity link-span was installed at 25 Berth in the Empress Dock. In 1977 No. 5 drydock (opened in 1895) was closed and filled in to provide a large storage area for all types of vehicles to the rear of 34/35 Berths.

The main shipping companies now involved in the movement of vehicles are the Swedish Wallenius Lines, Norwegian Hoegh Ugland Auto Liners (HUAL), Mitsui OSK Lines, Nippon Yusen Kaisha, TMM, AMF, Flota Suardiazi, Grimaldi and United European Car Carriers (UECC). The total number of vehicles passing through the Port in 1997 was 516,000, made up of 366,000 for export and 150,000 imports. A wide variety of vehicles are involved from Rover Cars, Ford, Honda, Renault, Jaguar, Nissan, General Motors and Land Rover, including tractors and various heavy vehicles. Many of these now arrive in the Docks by train.

Grain Traffic

Since Rank's established their Solent Flour Mills in the New Docks in 1934, grain has been regularly imported through 102/3 Berths using electrically operated pumps on the quayside which suck the grain from the ship's hold and transfer it to conveyor belts leading direct into the Mill, some 600 feet from the quayside.

During 1981 construction of a new grain export terminal was commenced at 47 Berth in the Ocean Dock for Continental (UK) Ltd. This was first used in August 1982. A second grain export terminal was built at 36 Berth on the River Itchen for Southampton Grain Silos (now Soufflet Grain Terminal Ltd), being officially opened by the Princess Royal in 1983. In 1987 additional silos were constructed on this site. The export of grain through the Port has gradually increased - shipments being made to Spain, Italy, Russia, Saudi Arabia and the Far East. An average of one million tonnes are exported annually.

The Windward Terminal which opened in 1993 at 101 Berth. The building includes 60,000 sq ft of temperature-controlled storage accommodation for bananas. The vessel is *Geest St Lucia*, which no longer operates on Geest Line service. The Line is now covered by chartered vessels. *Associated British Ports*

Wine

For many years South African wine arrived in barrels in Union Castle Line ships and were forwarded by rail to Nine Elms, which was one of the Southern Railway's goods depots in London. By the early 1960s the quantity being received each year was such that the South African Wine Farmers Association decided to have a new building built in the Western Docks. It was opened in October 1965. Several of the Union Castle ships were fitted with special tanks so that the wine could be carried in bulk for pumping ashore into road vehicles for the short distance to the new plant.

In 1974 Martini Rossi, now known as Bacardi Martini, opened a bulk storage and bottling depot in the Western Docks and subsequently took over the premises of the South African Wine Growers Association. The wine and spirits now arrive from Italy, Cyprus and the West Indies. In 1976 a pipeline was laid from Martini Rossi premises to 106/7 Berths so that the bulk wine tankers could discharge direct to the depot. Approximately 30 million litres are received annually for bottling and distribution throughout the UK.

Other Activities

The Transport Act of 1980 included provision for the privatisation of the British Transport Docks Board. This resulted in 1982 of the setting up of Associated British Ports and shares in the new company were offered for sale in February 1983.

In August 1984 a Free Trade Zone was established at 102 Berth in the Western Docks, but in October 1996 this was replaced by a new 8-acre purpose-built depot adjacent to the Container Terminal. This consolidated and expanded the Free Trade Zone facilities and the Port's container groupage services.

In 1989 the National Dock Labour scheme was abolished and this brought about ABP's withdrawal from cargoing and new arrangements. Private independent stevedoring companies such as Southampton Container Terminal Ltd, Southampton Cargo Handling PLC and Berkeley Handling Ltd. now provide the cargo handling facilities.

Towage services at Southampton are provided by several companies; Howard Smith Towage & Salvage and Red Funnel Group. Solent Towage provide two tugs with fire-fighting capability on a 24-hour basis at the Fawley Oil Terminal. Itchen Marine (Towage) Ltd. deal with the towage of small vessels and barges etc.

The Post Office Central Marine Depot at Southampton was opened in November 1974 on a five acre site at 203 Berth adjacent to the container berths in the Western Docks. In 1981 the section of the Post Office dealing with submarine cables was included in a new public corporation. BT Marine was formed as a wholly owned subsidiary on 1st October 1987. In 1994 BT Marine was taken over by Cable & Wireless who moved operations to Portland in Dorset at the end of 1997.

In 1985 a large transit shed at 26/7 Berth in the Empress Dock was used for dealing with the import of animal feed and fertiliser from the Continent. In 1991, however, this operation was transferred to 107 Berth where new facilities were provided, enabling larger ships to be

Left: Four of the straddle carriers supplied by the Finnish firm SISU Terminal Systems Inc. These carriers can stack one container over three.

Below: Operations room at the Container Terminal - considerable emphasis is placed on information technology to enhance the operations.

used for this traffic. Imports of soya, citrus and sunflower pellets from India, South America and the USA, plus fertilisers are part of this large traffic. A total of 304,600 tonnes were dealt with in 1996. In May 1995 a new 10,000 sq. metre terminal, known as the 'Mulberry Terminal' was opened, thereby providing increased storage capacity.

In 1991 a contract was signed with the Federation of Canary Islands Fruit Growers for handling vegetables and fruit from the islands. As a result a new terminal opened at 104 Berth - the Canary Fruit Terminal - consisting of 115,000 sq ft of storage space. In 1994 a new contract was signed under which all Canary Islands fruit imported to the UK would be handled exclusively at Southampton. In the following year a new cold storage extension, with a floor space of 14,200 sq metres, was brought into use at the Terminal. 133,000 tonnes of tomatoes, cucumbers, peppers, avocadoes and aubergines were handled during the winter of 1995/6. The cold store extension has also allowed for other fruit to be dealt with between May and October, outside the Canary Islands season.

Banana traffic was a welcome return to Southampton, when in February 1993 Geest PLC transferred their entire UK banana and shipping operations from Barry, South Wales to Southampton. To cater for this traffic, ABP provided, at 101 Berth, the Windward Terminal occupying a 9-acre site including 60,000 sq ft of temperature-controlled storage space and 20,000 sq ft of covered storage space for general cargo. A lorry park and container handling area, with weighbridge and associated facilities, is also provided. Almost 35% of the UK's banana trade passes through the Port, which together with the traffic from the Canary Islands, makes Southampton one of the largest fruit handling ports in the country.

In recent years the whole aspect of shipping worldwide has changed. Cargo handling has been fully mechanised and ships are turned round much quicker that in years gone by. With the final withdrawal of the car ferry services during 1984, Princess Alexandra Dock (formerly the Outer Dock) was no longer appropriate for commercial shipping and the 75-acre site was turned into the area now known as 'Ocean Village'. This area includes shops, houses, offices and a marina. The Town Quay, which for many years was the hub of coastwise shipping for the Port, has also been redeveloped, with offices and restaurants, together with another marina.

A new ABP office, named Ocean Gate, was brought into use near 45 Berth in the Ocean Dock in August 1991. The Port is also the home to Europe's leading centre for marine sciences - the Southampton Oceanography Centre, which was officially opened in April 1996 on a 13-acre site with access to the Empress Dock.

Despite investments totalling nearly £50million over the last ten years, there is still tremendous potential for expansion. In anticipation of considerable growth in the future, ABP has begun the consultation and planning process to bring its development area at Dibden Bay into operational use. This area is a reclaimed site directly opposite the existing port estate, formed from the dredgings of Southampton Water. It was acquired by the Port Authority in the 1960s for the purpose of future development. In consultation with local authorities and interest groups, ABP is examining the environmental and transportation issues to ensure that the development is carried out in a sensitive manner. Considerable foresight has been shown in developing the Port to date and after many years of being Britain's premier passenger port, it is now being developed into an extremely efficient cargo port. Associated British Ports have shown complete confidence in the future to ensure that the Port of Southampton will continue to be in the forefront of any future shipping developments well into the 21st century.

P&O have a long association with the Port. Here, *Colombo Bay* is seen arriving at the container terminal. *Associated British Ports*

Dock Managers 1835 - 1998

1835-1842		1936-1956	
Capt. W. Ward R.N.	Superintendent	R.P. Biddle	Docks & Marine Manager
1842-1852		(Between 1941 and 1945 Mr. R.P. Biddle was seconded	
G. Saintsbury	General Superintendent & Secretary	to the Ministry of Transport and during this period Mr.	
1852-1854		H.A. Short was Manager)	
Capt. G. Peacock	Superintendent & Dock Master	1956-1962	
1854-1892		S.A. Finnis	Chief Docks Manager
P. Hedger	Superintendent & Dock Master	1963-1964	
(This title was changed to Secretary and Superintendent		W.F. Griffiths	Chief Docks Manager
in 1874, when a separate Dock Master was appointed)		1964-1967	
1892-1901		D.A. Stringer	Chief Docks Manager
J. Dixon	Docks & Marine Superintendent	1967-1970	
1902-1920		E.A.C. Howells	Chief Docks Manager
T.M. Williams	Docks & Marine Superintendent	1970-1976	
(later changed to Docks & Marine Manager)		D.A. Stringer	Port Director
1920-1927		1977-1982	
Gilbert S. Szlumper	Docks & Marine Manager	J.B. Williams	Port Director
1927-1933		1982-1989	
George R. Newcombe	Docks & Marine Manager	W.D. Noddings	Port Director
1933-1936		1989-	
E.J. Missenden	Docks & Marine Manager	A. Kent	Port Manager

Top: An interesting photograph taken in September 1920 of the then Docks and Marine, Mr T.M. Williams in his office. The clutter of his office was very typical of the day.   *Associated British Ports*

Above: Her Majesty the Queen accompanied by Mr. D.A. Stringer, Port Director, in the Western Docks prior to Her Majesty embarking on the royal yacht *Britannia* on 7th August 1974.   *Associated British Ports*

Left: Mr R.P. Biddle (left), Docks & Marine Manager at Southampton from 1936 until 1956 welcomes John Elliot newly appointed chairman of the The Railway Executive (right) in May 1951.
          Associated British Ports courtesy Southampton City Museums

Above: Plenty of well loaded pleasure steamers accompanied Canadian Pacific's *Empress of Britain* up Southampton Water on 22nd June 1939 when their Majesties King George VI and Queen Elizabeth returned from their Canadian tour. The vessel in the centre is Red Funnel's tug/tender *Calshot*, now owned by Southampton City Council. The *Empress of Britain* was sunk on 28th October 1940, being the largest merchant ship lost by the Allies during the 1939/45 war. *Associated British Ports*

Right: Her Majesty Queen Elizabeth the Queen Mother with the previous Port Director Mr W.D. Noddings. The Queen Mother was a member of the Royal family who regularly travelled through the port on official and other occasions, such as on the day in 1939 in the picture above. *Associated British Ports*

Passenger & Cargo Tonnage

Passenger Numbers		Cargo Tonnage	
1892	122,108	1892	421,611
1913	378,917	1913	1,319,523
1923	414090	1923	1,009,976
1933	480627	1933	881,829
1938	560,426	1938	1,084,714
1950	561,318	1950	780,902
1956	626,856	1956	1,235,300
1962	515,137	1962	1,340,795
1969	484,217 + 675,573 (Cross Channel)	1969	1,633,592
1981	146,000 + 752,000 (Cross Channel)	1981	2,095,000
1987	121,738	1987	6,634,306
1992	164,833 + 508,142 (Cross Channel)	1992	6,225,500
1996	224,175 + 464,915 (Cross Channel)	1996	9,526,400
1997	211,510	1997	9,124,100

THE END – the mooring gang securing the ropes on the Cunarder *Sylvania* during the 1960s.

Associated British Ports courtesy Southampton City Museums